I Love School
Bedtime Healing Meditation for Children

Little Blue Zen

I Love School

Copyright@ 2024 Jo Galloway

The right of the author has been asserted to her following the copyright writing, designs and patent act of Australia.

All rights reserved. No part of this book may be reproduced, stored or transmitted by any means whether auditory, graphic, mechanical, or electronic without the written permission of the author. Unauthorised reproduction of any part of this work is illegal and is punishable by law.

Unless otherwise noted, the author and the publisher make no explicit guarantees as the accuracy of the information contained in this book may differ based on individual experiences and context

ISBN: 978-1-7635801-7-6

Published by Little Blue Zen
Birdwood NSW
Printed in Australia
Cover Design: Gagan Karunachandra
Editing: Kristine Gibson
jo@littlebluezen.com
http://www.littlebluezen.com

I Love School

Bedtime Healing Meditation for Children

Jo Galloway

Your child may like other books in this series

- Bully Proof. Keeping out the bullies.

- I am Different, I am Me.

- The Magical Treasure Hunt. Building Confidence.

- The Magical Worry Balloon.

- Angelic Dreams. Meet your Guardian Angel.

- Scared of the Dark.

- Bedwetting, Dry Nights.

- A Coat of Flying Colours

Little Blue Zen.com

INTRODUCTION

Why Healing Meditations

As children we make sense of our experiences based on our limited understanding and perception. We may misinterpret events or draw conclusions that form the basis of limiting beliefs that influence our entire life. These beliefs become ingrained over time, shaping our thoughts, feelings and behaviours well into adulthood unless consciously challenged.

In my work as a practising Hypnotherapist, I've found that all my clients' concerns, whether rooted in fears, feelings of inadequacy, addictive behaviours, or other challenges, trace back to their early childhood experiences, interactions, and upbringing. It's important to note that these issues don't exclusively stem from abusive or dysfunctional environments; limiting beliefs can arise from various circumstances.

Parents or caregivers wield substantial influence in shaping our perceptions of ourselves and the world around us. Remarks, criticisms, or comparisons made by family members can foster beliefs about our capabilities, worthiness, or potential. Furthermore, interactions with peers, teachers, and authority figures also contribute to the formation of these beliefs. Repeated experiences of rejection or failure can solidify beliefs such as "I'm not good enough" or "I'm unworthy of love."

This realisation ignited my passion for intervening at the source: working with children to prevent these beliefs from taking root and manifesting into significant challenges in adulthood. By addressing issues early on, we can guide children to develop into the best versions of themselves, free from the burden of limiting beliefs that could otherwise dominate their lives. .

How Healing Meditation will help your child.

Teaching children meditation offers a multitude of benefits that can positively influence their daily lives and overall development. A regular mindfulness meditation practice provides valuable tools for managing stress, navigating emotions, and promoting overall well-being. Healing meditations, in particular, bolster your child's self-belief, helping to remove any resistance they may face in adulthood. This leads to a happier, more successful and fulfilling life.

Unlike traditional meditation, which often centres on relaxation, healing meditations go a step further by focusing on recovery, balance, and reprogramming a child's self-belief. These meditations use techniques such as breathing exercises, visualization, and guided imagery to not only foster deep relaxation but also reshape their mindset.

This targeted approach helps build a stronger sense of self-confidence and resilience. By integrating positive affirmations and emotional healing, healing meditations offer a distinct advantage over traditional methods, laying a powerful foundation for a child's future success and well-being.

Meditation can also be an effective part of your child's bedtime routine, helping to calm the mind and prepare the body for restful sleep. Techniques like guided imagery and deep breathing, as outlined in this book, can signal to the brain that it's time to wind down.

Sharing these calming moments at bedtime not only strengthens the bond between parent and child, but also creates a supportive and nurturing environment. It also sets a positive example, emphasizing the importance of self-care and mindfulness.

With patience and consistency, you can help your child develop a lifelong practice that supports their mental, emotional, and physical health. Give your child the gift of relaxation and imagination with this easy-to-read story designed to inspire and uplift.

I Love School

I LOVE SCHOOL is a beautifully crafted meditation journey designed to guide children through a soothing experience that fosters relaxation and a positive mindset about school. The journey begins with a gentle visualization where children imagine themselves climbing a set of heavenly stairs filled with sparkling stars in a fantastical playground. This imagery helps them drift into a state of calmness and ease, setting the stage for a restful and soothing experience.

This enlighten meditation introduces the concept of a "special brain"—a metaphorical spaceship that responds to their thoughts and words. This special brain is portrayed as a powerful vessel that delivers the experiences and feelings they focus on. By illustrating how negative thoughts about school can generate negative feelings and experiences, the meditation encourages children to shift their mindset toward positivity.

Through a series of positive affirmations and self-talk exercises, the meditation gently guides children to replace limiting beliefs (such as "I hate school" or "I'm not good enough") with uplifting and empowering statements like "I love school" and "I am smart." This process is designed to boost their self-confidence and foster a more positive relationship with their educational experience.

The meditation emphasizes the transformative power of positive thinking, showing children how adopting an optimistic perspective can make their school experience more enjoyable and rewarding. It encourages them to see school as a place of opportunity and growth, reinforcing that their attitude and mindset play a crucial role in shaping their daily experiences and overall well-being.

I LOVE SCHOOL is a nurturing tool that not only helps children relax but also empowers them to approach school with enthusiasm and confidence, turning it into a more engaging and positive part of their lives. Delivered in a slow, monotone voice, this story captivates and soothes.

I Love School

Hello, my lovable Little Starlight.

Are you ready for a wonderful adventure?

Before we begin, make yourself comfortable.

Have a little wiggle to settle in.

Uncross your legs and place your hands gently by your side.

Perfect!

When you're ready, keep your head still and look up.

Focus your eyes on a spot on the ceiling above you.

That's right.
Now take a deep, slow breath in.
Keep looking up.
As you breathe out, softly close your eyes.
Perfect!
As your eyes gently close, feel your body relax.
Your eyes are becoming so sleepy.
Your body is sinking comfortably into your warm, comfy bed.
So let's try that one more time, shall we?
Roll your eyes up and keep looking up.
Take a deep breath in, feeling your eyes wanting to close.

Every time you blink, you're relaxing even more.

Now breathe out and softly close your eyes.

That's right.

Now, forget all about your eyes and feel a drifting, floating feeling in your body.

You can see perfectly well with your eyes closed because all boys and girls have the most wonderful imaginations.

Way better than grown-ups.

Now envision yourself standing in a magical playground.

You know it is magical because bright dazzling rainbows are all around you.

The rainbows are casting vibrant colours everywhere you look as they twirl and shimmer through the air.

Through the shimmer of colour, you can see the swings, the monkey bars and a seesaw.

As if by magic, a sparkling stairway of stars appears, reaching high into the sky.

The stairs seem to go on forever!

You tilt your head back to see just how far they go.

You take a step closer to get a better look and feel that the starry stairs are inviting you to start your journey.

You're feeling both brave and excited as you prepare to climb up, one step at a time.

Here you go—step onto the first star.

Just like magic, the star turns a bright, warm red.

Stand there for a moment and let that warm red colour fill you up from your feet.

Now step up to the next star.

As you do, the stars shimmer and change colour from red into a beautiful orange.

Your feet begin to feel warm and tingly as they soak up the lovely orange light.

The next step is waiting for you.

As you step onto it, the star instantly turns into bright, golden-yellow sunshine.

Feel the sunshine rush up from the star into your tummy, filling you with a powerful sense of calm.

Now you step up to the next star, almost floating onto it.

Suddenly, the star turns a radiant green.

The colour rushes into your feet, up your legs, filling your tummy and chest.

Feel your whole chest come alive with joy.

With your eyes closed, let this vibrant green colour fill your heart with happiness.

Feeling very sleepy now, you step up onto the next star.

As you do, the colour instantly changes to a soothing blue, relaxing you more and more.

On the next step, the star turns a deep purple.

Stay still for a moment and imagine the purple filling your head with a sense of calm and peace, making you feel sleepier and sleepier.

You're at the top now, so step up onto the last star.

Once you've placed both feet on this last star, turn around and sit down.

From here, you can see the entire world below.

You notice the heavenly clouds floating softly, angels gliding gently, and golden rainbows arching across the sky.

Stars shimmer in a pure, white light, creating a magical glow around you.

As you sit on top of this enchanted stairway of stars, you feel a tingling sensation from the top of your head to the tips of your toes, enveloping you in shimmering white light.

Below, you see other children playing happily.

Sitting atop this magical stairway, you feel completely safe and deeply happy.

As you sit quietly, you hear a gentle voice.

"Do you know how special and clever you are?" the voice asks.

"Did you know you have a super cool brain that listens to every word you say and every thought you think?

Your words and thoughts are like tiny spaceships that zoom out into the universe and bring back whatever you're thinking or talking about.

"So, if you keep saying or thinking sad things about yourself," the voice continues, those little spaceships think this is what you want and will fly out into the universe and bring back the same sad feelings."

For example, if you say, "I don't like school" or "school is boring," those cosmic spaceships will zoom out and bring back those same unhappy feelings about school. Sometimes, you might have thoughts like:

"My teachers are always picking on me."

"I can't focus; I'm not as smart as the other kids."

"I keep forgetting things, and nobody likes me."

"I have a test coming up and I know I'm going to fail."

"I'm not good enough."

"I not smart, and I just don't like school."

Or maybe you even say, "I hate school, and I don't want to go."

Because your special brain loves you so much, it wants to give you whatever you ask for.

It listens to everything you say and think, and it's always ready to send out your little spaceships into the universe.

These spaceships will bring back exactly what you're thinking about.

If you think I'm going to fail my exams, you will fail your exams.

So, if you keep saying things like "I hate school," your special brain might send back reasons to make school feel even worse.

Like bullies, tough exams, or feeling like you have no friends and forget things.

Your special brain doesn't know the difference between right and wrong, good and bad, or truth and untruth.

It only knows what you tell it.

It will give you everything it thinks you want based on your words and thoughts.

Now you see just how clever your special brain is.

By changing your thoughts and words, you can transform your entire world and make school fun!

Think of one thing you love about school. Everyone has one special thing they really enjoy.

Maybe you like sports, or your friends, math, or reading books, or even playtime.

When you focus on all the good things, your special spaceships will zoom out and bring you back even more of the things you enjoy.

So, instead of waking up tomorrow and saying, "I hate school," try saying, "I love school, and school is fun."

Instead of saying, "I can't do that; it's too hard," say, "I can do anything!" and "I am so clever and smart!".

"I am here to do amazing things!"

Instead of feeling like you're not good enough, say to yourself, "I am perfect, I am capable, and I am confident."

Remind yourself, "I have lots of fantastic friends," and "school is fun."

Thinking about all the good things will bring even more good things into your life.

If you believe you are smart, you'll be smart.

If you think the exam is easy, it will be easy.

Tell yourself, "I love to study," and "I am a winner."

Your teachers and parents will be so proud of you for changing your thoughts and words.

Your spaceships are doing cartwheels in the sky, because they're thrilled to bring you good things and feelings of happiness.

As everything becomes easier, you will amaze your friends.

They might say, "Wow, what happened to you?"

You can tell them, "I changed my words."

"When I use happy words, I get happy days."

I have also changed the way I think.

I stopped saying, "I'm going to fail," or even thinking, "I'm never going to succeed."

Instead, I say, "I'm going to win," "I am the best," "I am the smartest," and "I am a whizz kid."

Every day I remind myself, "I can do anything!"

Every day, I say, "I love to study," "Studying is easy," and "School is great."

I tell myself, "I focus, concentrate, and learning is fun."

I never forget to say, "I love to read, I love to write, and school days are the best!"

How wonderful it is to know that when you change your words and thoughts, you can change your entire world around you.

That is exactly how clever you truly are.

You can choose to think, "This is hard," or you can choose to think, "This is easy."

Whatever you choose, your magical cosmic spaceship will bring you.

When you sit down for a test or exam, you choose to think, "Wow, this is so easy."

"I am smart; I am a winner."

Instead of saying "I can't," you now say, "I can."

Changing the way you think will change the way you feel.

Changing the way you think about going to school will change how you feel about going to school.

It's really that simple.

Now you know how to talk to your special brain.

Every day can be a great day.

You love going to school, and in the morning, you'll jump out of bed excited and happy.

Fill your brilliant special brain with positive thoughts.

Tell all your friends, "I love school," and "school is the best."

You love being positive—no more Negative Nellies live here!

Now you know how to talk to your special brain.

Every day is a great day.

You love going to school.

So now, my Little Starlight, it is time to softly drift off to sleep.

Feeling excited to wake up in the morning and go to school.

Tonight, you will dream the most magical dreams about your special brain and your amazing spaceships.

Good night, my amazing Little Starlight. Sweet dreams!

A Coat of Flying Colours

Sitting exams can often bring to the surface a child's self-sabotaging beliefs of I am not good enough, fears of failure or fear of rejection, along with bucket loads of anxiety.

Wearing the magical coat of Flying Colours is like wearing Superman's cape. This coat will transform your child's inner beliefs, allow access to their phenomenal memory, and enable them to remain calm and in total control while undertaking any exam.

Allow this gentle healing meditation to ease their worries, enhance their belief in their capabilities, empower their positivity to pass every exam with flying colours.

I LOVE SCHOOL is also available on YouTube, providing a soothing auditory experience children can enjoy at home, in the car, or anywhere they need a moment of relaxation."

Listen on YouTube

www.ingramcontent.com/pod-product-compliance
Lightning Source LLC
Chambersburg PA
CBHW042356070526
44585CB00028B/2948